I

BREAKING UP IS HARD TO DO

BUT YOU COULD'VE DONE BETTER

Stories from People

Cartoons by Hilary Fitzgerald Campbell

A N M A L

BREAKING UP IS HARD TO DO
but you could've done better

Animal Media Group books may be ordered through booksellers
or by contacting:

Animal Media Group
100 1st Ave suite 1100
Pittsburgh, PA 15222
www.animalmediagroup.com
421-566-5656

Cover art: Hilary Campbell.
Back cover art: Hilary Campbell.

ISBN: 978-0-9974315-4-4
ISBN: 978-0-9974315-5-1

DEDICATION

To that one dude,
for being such an inspirational dick.

♥

INTRODUCTION

I assume you've been broken up with or you've broken up with someone or maybe you know somebody who got dumped last weekend in the worst way possible and you're like "wow, that sucks." And if none of those apply, I'm absolutely positive you've been ghosted. I know this because people are terrible. This book has proven to me that people are terrible. People are terrible and they do terrible things to each other and yet still we wake up every morning and we have hope that maybe someday someone won't be so terrible, but in the meantime at least there's always more toast.

This book didn't start out as a book. This started out as me crying on a freeway overpass in Brooklyn, moping around for some time, and thinking I'd better draw about this (because that's what I do).

I drew one cartoon and laughed. It helped.

And if I laughed, maybe other people could too. Maybe they would be willing to share their heartbreak with me and I could draw something and we could chuckle and be relieved and also have a little silent sweet revenge in anonymously exposing our exes' idiocy. Would people be into that?

The answer is yes. It must be, because you're holding a book of those sad sad stories with the pictures that I drew. So thank you for buying this, really. It kinda makes me think you're not so terrible except for the fact that all people are terrible. Flip through, you'll see.

Love on, love wild, love free,

Hilary

She said to me,
"You're someone I want to marry,
not someone I want to date."

Men for
now

Men for
later

had been seeing this guy long distance for about a year. We were such kindred spirits that we could actually use the distance to our advantage; we'd have long, intimate phone calls late into the night, during which no topic was off-limits. We even successfully managed to keep open sex lives with other people and not get jealous or weird.

Before one of his visits, he wanted to discuss how we were both feeling about things. I gave it some thought and realized I loved him, but that I liked being open. I also liked that he was able to be open. I was happy.

So, I told him I loved him, but defined it as "caring" about him and was careful to explain that I wanted the relationship to stay as it was. He said he cared about me too, but didn't want to use the word "love." Fair enough, I thought. When he arrived, we spent the weekend completely wrapped up in each other, having awesome sex and conversation.

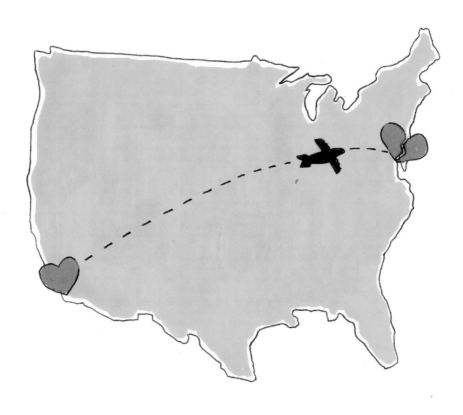

So I was pretty surprised when upon my arrival in his city a couple months later -- after buying plane tickets, taking time off work, and renting an expensive hotel room -- he'd decided that the word "love" made him so uncomfortable that he didn't want to have sex with me anymore.

When I was in college, I broke up with my boyfriend of two years.

I felt like it had been a long time coming. But when I told him it was over, he threw a Game Boy at my head and ran off into the streets barefoot. I've never been more confused in my life.

HE THREW A GAME BOY AT
MY HEAD

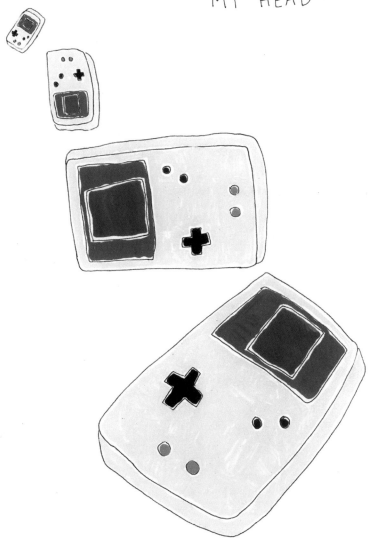

broke up with my eighth-grade girlfriend because
I wanted to spend more time with my dog. The
Kids ridiculed me at school, but it was still the best
decision I ever made.

THIS DOG

NEEDS YOU

We dated for a year, which is like an eternity for a high school freshman. Then the Regina George of our town IM'd me, saying she made out with him in a closet during second period. I broke up with him later, also over IM, and he replied, "I still luv ya." We almost got back together, until I saw him making out with an older girl in between classes. He continued to pursue me through cyberspace until junior year of high school - there were Dashboard Confessional lyrics in my away message for months.

Now he's fat and I'm getting my PhD.

broke up with my boyfriend and then realized I had made a huge mistake.

When I asked if we could talk it through, he said he needed some time to think things over, but finally agreed to meet me at his apartment a few days later.

The whole way over in the car, I practiced a speech about how wrong I had been. I had just been going through a rough spot, I would tell him. My unhappiness had nothing to do with him or our relationship. I even typed the speech into my phone's Notepad app and walked around the block a few times, reciting it. We sat across from each other in silence for a while at his dining room table, like spouses waiting for their lawyers to arrive to finalize divorce.

Then the conversation went something like this:

Me: "This time apart has made me realize that I don't need you in my life. But it's also made me realize that I want you in my life."

This was followed by me listing the things that I still liked about him.

Him: "Well, I also came to some conclusions during these last few days. And I'm sorry, but I really think we should end this. I think... I'm just no longer physically attracted to you."

Me: "Okay... back to the dating sites we go, I guess."

Him: "Well, you should probably take a few months to get over this."

Me: "I think I'll be fine."

Him: "Also, you should shower more."

Me: "..."

ARE YOU GETTING DUMPED TODAY?

a flowchart

I MEAN, PROBABLY

WHY WOULD YOU ASK ME THAT

YOU NEED TO CHILL

I DK, MAYBE NOT

YOU BROUGHT IT UP YOU OBVIOUSLY WANNA TALK ABOUT IT

SORRY, NEVERMIND

...

YOU'RE RIGHT, THANK YOU

WHEN HAVE YOU EVER BEEN CHILL

THEN AGAIN, THAT LAST TEXT DIDN'T HAVE ANY EXCLAMATION MARKS & THERE'S USUALLY AT LEAST TWO

I MEAN, YES

NOTHING EVEN HAPPENED THOUGH

THEY'RE SO OVER ME

WHEN THERE'S WINE

OK I'M BUYING WINE

A TEXT!

IS THERE WINE?

I JUST GOT DUMPED

He wasn't a great boyfriend, to say the least. After two years of dating, the only gift he ever gave me was a set of black lingerie for Christmas.

When we broke up, the talk was surprisingly going okay. Until he asked, "Can you give me back that lingerie I gave you?"

the one
you wear
literally
every day

the one
he bought you
& now wants
back

the one
for
"exercising"

My first real girlfriend in high school wasn't very good to me. It got off to a rocky start when I asked her out several times and she kept rejecting me.

When she finally said yes, I thought everything would be great. But it wasn't: I was just starting to develop a friendship with a new girl who was so much kinder to me. When my girlfriend went with her family to New York for winter break, I was stuck in our hometown, hanging out with my friends and this new girl.

One day, the new girl confessed she liked me. I was ecstatic. But I also felt bound by my pious high school standards of commitment and chivalry, so I asked if she could wait for me. Unfortunately, we were teenagers and she wanted a first kiss on New Year's Eve. I had a problem.

So I left a message on my girlfriend's home message machine saying how I felt, which at the

IF YOU PRESS PLAY YOU DON'T
HAVE A BOYFRIEND ANYMORE

time seemed like a logical idea. I knew it was cowardly. But I told myself it was okay because we could have a conversation when she got back. Heck, I would even wait for that conversation to happen before I moved forward with my new relationship!

Well, my phone finally rang. I took a deep breath and squeaked "hello," ready to take the abuse. "Hey!" she replied. She was in a car on the way home from the airport with her family. She told me how New York helped clear her mind, how she realized what an awful person she had been to me, and how much she really cared about me. She told me about all the gifts she got me while she was there. I felt sick.

She was almost home and asked if she could call me back once she settled. "Sure," I said. Fuck. Ten minutes go by, and then I see my phone vibrating. It's a text from her, very long and explicit, basically saying, "you are an asshole."

HOW TO RUIN YOUR LIFE

- NEVER TRY AN AVOCADO
- MISS THE BUS (REPEATEDLY)
- FALL IN LOVE

I broke up with my high school boyfriend, because, well, he was dumb and inappropriately old for me. A week or so after we broke up, I came home (to my parents' house, because I was sixteen) to find a Manila envelope on my doorstep.

Inside I found my "South Park" T-shirt with Eric Cartman screaming, "I want cheesy poofs!" on it, which he had borrowed from me, and a floppy disk.

Yes, a floppy disk -- because he thought he was so good with computers and it was 2006. His final letter to me, telling me what I bitch I was and how I'd never do better than him, was on a floppy disk.

reluctantly dated this very nice, chubby trumpet player my freshman year of art school. I could tell he was feeling it a lot more than I was. But every time I tried to break up with him, he would cry until I took it back. It was kind of a disaster.

I went up to Canada when summer break started, and my darling boyfriend decided to visit me. My father was driving up for my birthday, so the trumpet player hitched a ride and they drove up together, sharing the wheel for most of the ten-hour drive.

During his visit, he snooped through my computer and read some passages he didn't like in my online diary (this was back in the days of LiveJournal) and proceeded to cry every chance he got for the rest of the week.

The night before he was supposed to drive back down to the States with my dad, I'd had enough. I said we should take a break for the rest of the summer,

GIRL DUMPS BOY

DAD DRIVES BOY HOME

. . .

DAD TOTALS CAR

because clearly we weren't making each other happy. Four hours into their drive the next day, with my trumpeter behind the wheel, the car fishtailed on the highway and rolled three times. Both men ended up in the hospital and my dad's beloved Volvo was totaled.

They had to wait in the hospital for my freshly exed boyfriend's parents to drive the remaining six hours to pick them up and then drive them all home again.

Sorry, Dad.

$$\frac{\text{OVER}}{\text{UNDER}} \times \text{YOU} = \text{LOL MATH IDK I'M SAD}$$

was out of town and he went drinking. He decided to do the "chivalrous" thing and drive his cocktail waitress home. He got a DUI and felt "obligated" to sleep with the cocktail waitress to thank her for bailing him out. Oh, and he wanted my engagement ring back so he could pay his legal fees.

A GUIDE TO CHIVALRY

1. Get drunk at bar while fiancé is out of town (totally harmless)

2. Offer to give lady who helped you get drunk a ride home (so generous)

3. Get DUI on way there (whoops!)

4. After she bails you out (she will), sleep with her as a nice thank you (it's the right thing to do!)

5. Ask fiancé to give back her engagement ring to cover legal fees (obviously)

Her name was Emily and she was visiting me at Moody Bible Institute, an ultra-fundamentalist school in Chicago, where I was desperately trying to believe in Jesus.

We were both virgins, as God had intended, and we both subscribed to the belief that sex of any kind before marriage was deeply sinful. Even masturbation. Especially masturbation.

We had been struggling to stick to our carefully mapped out physical boundaries in the attempt to stay pure. We were doing stuff like dry humping in public parks since my dorm was rigorously gender-segregated.

On the night before she flew home, we were making out on the beach. I placed her hand on my crotch and started to grind. Within moments I was ejaculating into my shorts, in full daylight, on Oak Street Beach.

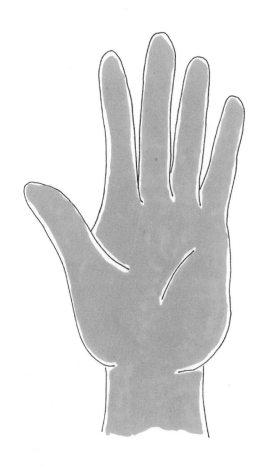

THIS HAND IS CLEAN
(BUT YOUR CONSCIENCE ISN'T)

I walked back to campus in my damp underwear, full of shame, swearing I would never tell anyone. As soon as I got on the elevator, my friend Jack asked what was wrong. Feeling as though God was testing me, I confessed everything. Within minutes, Jack gathered other faithful worshippers to the intervention. "If you keep dating this girl," they said, "she's going to destroy your walk with God."

That night, I called her and told her that what we had done was sinful, and that it was over between us. She was understandably furious. She pointed out that I was the one who pressured her into the crotch-rub to begin with. Being the holier-than-thou slut shamer I was, however, I was not willing to even discuss it.

I broke up with a girl for giving me a hand job. It wasn't even a real hand job.

I broke up with a boyfriend of five years on a Tuesday morning before work. We were arguing and it just came out. I went to work in tears, figuring we'd keep talking that evening.

That afternoon, I received a call from the security guard at the front desk of my office building. My boyfriend, in an attempt to humiliate me at work, had grabbed everything I owned from our apartment and was dumping it.

I took the elevator down to the lobby and saw my books, toiletries, photos, clothes, and mattress in an overwhelming heap. I plainly remember watching my boss step over a pair of my underwear to get to the exit door. That was definitely the end of us.

UP, PLEASE

Me: "I have to go home for a few weeks."

Him: "I kissed someone else on New Year's."

Me: "Oh. I have Mono."

OLD GIRLFRIEND

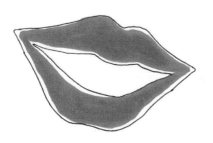

NEW GIRLFRIEND

My college boyfriend broke up with his previous girlfriend upon finding out that she had cheated on him with four different guys. Not on four occasions, but consistently over the whole span of their relationship.

Somehow, though, she still considered herself the wronged party, and when she found out that he had a new girlfriend (me), she called to tell him that she had tested positive for HIV/AIDS. He and I now probably have it too, she said.

We got tested, wept, and waited for our results. They were negative, of course. She sent a follow-up text a few weeks later that said something like, "How was the clinic? LOL."

She had AIDS pranked us!

While I knew the end was coming with one ex in particular, I also knew I wouldn't go down easy. I endured many humiliating days of the silent treatment from him, while I continued to deliver plates of chocolate cookies to his house and send texts and calls that went unanswered.

Struck by an especially pathetic idea during one of my grovels, I jumped on him, plastering my face against his chest and wrapping my legs around him like a baby marsupial, refusing to let go.

Oh, you want to leave me, do you? Well try driving away with a 130-pound human giving you a frontwards piggyback. Not gonna happen.

As I clung to him, crying my eyes out, afraid to be left, he just kept softly, patiently repeating, "I gotta go... I've just gotta go now."

YOU WANT
TO LEAVE
?

While in college, I spent a summer in New York City for an internship. I had just started dating someone I met at school while she was on her college visit trip, so she was technically still in high school, eighteen years old, and living with her parents in Ohio. Sue me.

While I was flying back and forth to Ohio, I met this other girl in NYC, Jes. I decided that flying to Ohio all the time sucked, and I didn't want to do it anymore. I called the Ohio girl to break up with her; she was blindsided and totally devastated. She was like, "What does this girl give you that I don't? Whatever it is, I'll figure out a way to give it to you!"

At that moment, I was walking to meet friends for sushi. I had recently discovered sushi and thought it was the best thing ever. So I replied, "You know how much I love sushi? Well, in New York I discovered muffins. They're easy. They're low

Circle one:

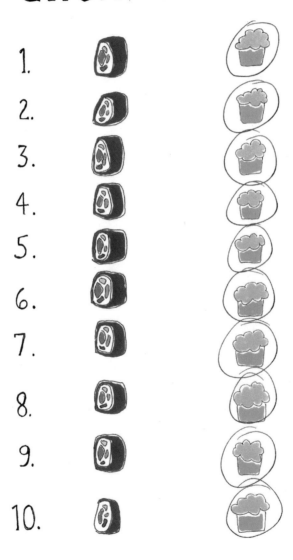

1.

2.

3.

4.

5.

6.

7.

8.

9.

10.

commitment. So even if I'm walking to a sushi restaurant, and I know that sushi is what I really want and the thing that will satisfy my hunger and is best for my body ... even knowing all of that, if I pass by a muffin in a window, I am going to stop in and eat that muffin. Even though I know that doing so is short-sighted and impulsive and will ruin my chance at sushi. I will stop and eat that muffin - not seven times out of ten, not eight times out of ten, not nine times out of ten. Ten times out of ten, I am going to eat the muffin." And then I hung up on her.

The muffin girl turned out to be a monster.

HAPPINESS
IS FLEETING
SO IS CEREAL

(HAVE ANOTHER BOWL
WHILE YOU STILL CAN)

When I was in junior high, a boy broke up with me because Jesus came to him in a vision and told him I was a whore.

My ex-girlfriend was a total princess - the daughter of a tycoon worth $500 million. We dated secretly for almost two years because she was afraid her dad wouldn't approve.

On top of that, she also had Bipolar disorder, rising to extreme highs that produced intense passion and falling to lows that would manifest in destructive manipulation. I realized I couldn't be in a secret relationship or handle the drama any longer, so I broke up with her.

She freaked out and threatened me, swearing she would go to the authorities and claim I did something bad to her unless I left the city we were living in. I had to give her a fake cell phone number I'd gotten from a different city to convince her I'd gone.

Six months after we broke up, while I was in a new and happy relationship, she found out that I was still around. She paid a guy to pretend to

50

become friends with me, then lure me into a meeting at a KFC, where she ambushed me.

Over the next hour, she told me how much she hated me. How much she loved me. How much she wished we were never together. And then... she proposed to me. She asked me to marry her and leave my new girlfriend. I said no.

Then she tried to kiss me, and I palmed her in the face and ran away. She grabbed my shirt and pulled me back to try again. I palm-pushed her face back again. This time I slipped away and ran into a waiting cab.

She emailed me for two weeks asking to get back together. I said no but that I forgave her for everything and I hoped she could forgive me. She emailed me one last time, cursing me to damnation for all eternity.

In college, I had been dating this guy for a few months; he was a sophomore and I was a junior. On the last day of the school year as we were saying our goodbyes, he said to me, "Okay, we're history."

I told my friend who had introduced us, and she said, "No he just meant, like, for now."

But no, that was it. Period. We were history.

THIS IS US

once broke it off with a guy who got pissed at me for spraining my ankle on our way to dinner before seeing a movie. He told me I'd wasted his Saturday night and refused to drive me to the hospital for an x-ray. Total Prince Charming.

YOU WASTED MY SATURDAY
NIGHT

needed to break up with my girlfriend. It was time: we were young, and it was just not going to last.

She kneed me in the balls. I fell to the ground. She stormed into her house. I got up and climbed into my car to drive home. She ran outside and jumped on the hood of my car, begging me not to leave. I got her off my car and drove home.

She started calling my cell phone nonstop, then called my parents' landline, thinking I might be there. My father, whose voice is very similar to mine, answered. She thought he was me and threatened to commit suicide.

Her parents forced her to go to therapy for years. I still get text messages from her about every six months telling me how much she hates me.

WARNING!

BREAK UP MAY RESULT IN:

KNEE-IN-BALLS

EX-TOSSING-THEMSELVES UPON-YOUR-CAR

EX-CALLING-YOUR-DAD-MISTAKING-HIM-FOR-YOU

was in the fifth grade and he was in the sixth. We would have these long phone conversations where I stretched the cord from the kitchen wall into the bathroom for privacy.

Once while on the phone with him, I was drinking orange soda and he made me laugh so hard that I threw up on the mouthpiece. That sucked. My dad had to put a lock on the phone.

He wanted to kiss me, but I wasn't ready. Then he met Kelly Powell - she was a slutty pastor's daughter from the next town over, and she was willing to give up the tongue all damn day.

He broke up with me on the playground. He and his douchebag friends chased after me, screaming the refrain, "Powell Power!" I cried.

But whatever, joke's on him. I became a super big slut three years later.

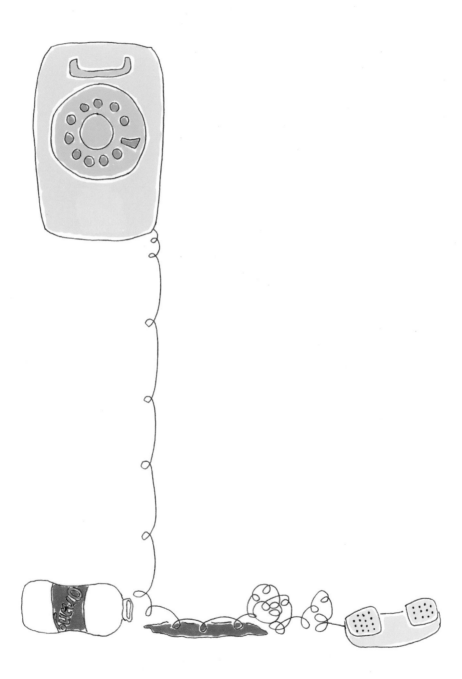

My high school boyfriend/first love of my life/first sexual everything broke up with me when he left for college. He said long distance would be too difficult.

For the next year we had this awful on-again off-again relationship where we still visited each other and said I love you and had explosive fights in parking lots.

Fast forward to me going to his college because I thought it would solve all of our problems. He said he didn't want to do long distance, right? I move into the dorms. We hook up once and I realize we're not dating. This isn't what I wanted. He refuses to have the talk with me in person; I end things with him over a Facebook message.

Okay, here's the kicker, and the reason I'm still talking about it in therapy five years later. The next summer, I find out he'd been dating a girl from our hometown - a girl I really liked and

SHE
ALSO
LOOKS
GOOD
IN
MY
SHIRTS

considered a friend - for at least six months behind my back. And there was overlap.

She was a year younger than me and they somehow made long distance work. Hmm.

This girl ended up being my fucking shadow. Everything I did, she did the next year. Artist and writer. Check. Emphasis in performance art and installations. Check. Biggest prize given by the art department. Check. Being in the same shows. Having to see her in classes regularly. Having to see her wearing my ex's shirts, which I had also worn on my own body. Check, check, check, motherfucking check.

Graduating and not having to see either of them was awesome. I was getting ready to move to Berlin to start a new chapter in my life.

Before leaving, I had coffee with a friend to catch up. When I brought up the move she said, "Oh, that's great!" Then she paused. "You know who you should talk to?"

Guess who else was moving to Berlin? Kill me now.

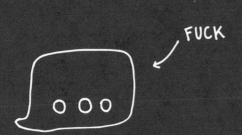

FUCK

On New Year's Eve, I get a text from my long-distance boyfriend around 8 p.m. - "Hey, so, I'm sorry but I really want to start the new year fresh."

My boyfriend of three years left a note and a pathetic flower in a beer bottle at my doorstep. He wrote that he was going to his ex-girlfriend's, which was hundreds of miles away, to "pick up some of his stuff."

My girlfriend broke up with me on our two-year anniversary. Before it happened, I had planned to give her a custom engraved picture frame (Happy Anniversary!) with a bunch of photos of us in it and a bottle of wine.

When shit hit the fan and we were both crying, I gave her the picture frame to show her what I'd planned. She held it gingerly, remorsefully, before I took it back.

"Isn't it beautiful?" I said before I threw the wine bottle up in the air, catching it by the neck and slamming it down like a sledgehammer on the picture frame. Glass and photos flew everywhere. I left the whole mess in the street before heading inside to polish off a new bottle in misery. Shattered love.

A guy I had been casually dating for months made plans with me on a Friday night to come over for dinner. He called to say he was early while I was getting ready, so I let him into the apartment and went back into my room to finish getting ready for dinner.

He followed me in, sat down and said, "We need to talk. I can't be in this relationship anymore."

First of all, I was unaware we were in a relationship! Second, you don't plan dinner with someone, then break up with her BEFORE SHE EATS.

He kept asking me how I was, like I was going to fall apart, until I had to kick him out. I texted my friends and made new plans to drink wine and eat pizza; I was already half ready, after all, and I wasn't about to mope.

REAPPROPRIATED PIZZA
(IS STILL PIZZA)

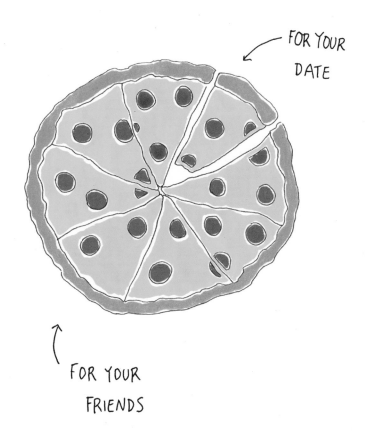

FOR YOUR
DATE

FOR YOUR
FRIENDS

My live-in boyfriend texted me asking if we could hang out that night, even though we hadn't planned to. On my way home to see him, I stopped at the grocery store to pick up some stuff. He texted again and asked me to buy some toothpaste for him while I was there.

Fifteen minutes later, he broke up with me... and took the toothpaste with him.

When the final Harry Potter movie was in theaters, my boyfriend of two years and I made plans to see it. I was coming from work, so we met at the theater in two separate cars for a late night showing.

I sobbed through the whole thing because I thought it was so amazing, and felt that it marked the end of an era for me. He laughed at my tears. Then we got in the car and he patted me on the shoulder like a condescending father (there, there, kiddo).

I wiped my eyes and said, "I'm not crying because Harry Potter is over, I'm crying because you and I are over." I was tired of how he trivialized my feelings in all situations. My declaration was liberating.

I got into my own car and drove away, watching him grow smaller in the rear-view mirror. The Boy Who Lived inspired me to be The Girl Who Left!

Dead Boyfriend, which is what I call him now, called me on Christmas Eve to tell me he met someone at work that week, was in love, and was moving with her to Nashville to support her modeling career. We had been together for almost six years.

Turns out she wasn't a model. She was a stripper and was wanted by her previous employer for stealing from the cash register. The moment they got to Nashville, she stole his car and every last cent. He called, crying. I didn't pick up and never spoke to him again.

That was four years ago, and Dead Boyfriend will still drunk dial me, broke and lonely. It's only funny when he leaves the message, "I just miss your voice."

SALE

BUY ONE GET ONE

FEATURED ITEM

The "Dead Boyfriend" Tee

Description:

For the Ex who will never be spoken of again, the "Dead Boyfriend" tee sees the truth faster than he ever could, because he is an idiot.

FRONT

SEE MORE:
BACK

Size:

S M L

Color:

ADD TO CART

He broke up with me on the car ride home, when I picked him up from the airport after Thanksgiving.

You're not welcome, by the way.

ARRIVALS ←   HE IS GOING TO
              DUMP YOU
              ↓   DEPARTURES →

THANKS FOR PICKING ME UP

This guy broke up with me at a party after a heated dispute over a movie trailer (which I was right about).

Fired up and petulant because he was wrong and he knew it, he took me into the other room and dumped me in the loudest, meanest way.

After he left the room, I went to gather my stuff and realized I left my shoes in the living room. When I called his name through the door he didn't answer. I had to make my way through the living room to grab my shoes, braving the stares of all the partiers who'd just overheard the entire scene.

He ghosted me after that. He was an idiot, so I know I'm better off. But also like, come on, my shoes!

YOU

GUY WHO JUST DUMPED YOU & ALL OF HIS DRUNK FRIENDS

OTHER STUFF

YOUR SHOES

LONG-EST WALK OF YOUR LIFE

tried to break up with him for three days in a row. He was kind of a droopy wallflower. As much as I love backpacking, sleeping on the ground, and cooking my own food, I also like a good Sancerre out of a decent wine glass, a gourmet burger, a nice massage, and the W Hotel. Different strokes for different folks.

We were also still not talking about being exclusive, and I got bored. So I told him, "This isn't working for me. You have emotional baggage and I just can't hang because it's wasting my time." Meanwhile I'm thinking to myself, shit, my eggs are dying.

His response was, "Let's just talk about it." I said no, we can't talk about it. We are talking about it right now. My bags were packed and I was leaving town! I left and he texted me that he wanted to make it work, and he's just been in a funk. "I've made up my mind," I replied. "Best of luck, you are a great guy, blah blah blah."

WHAT TYPE OF BAGGAGE DO YOU HAVE?

TRAVEL

EMOTIONAL

was dating this guy on and off for a year. He was
gorgeous, a real ladies' man, but I felt pretty sure he
only had eyes for me.

Eventually I got paranoid because I noticed he
was constantly commenting on girls' Instagram and
Facebook pictures with emoji hearts. Freaking emoji
hearts? And he would never comment on mine!

Then there was one girl in particular I suspected
he was talking to. My paranoia eventually led me to
stalk her on Twitter. She posted a picture from his
apartment. A condom wrapper was in the picture. Her
caption read: "Barely working this Saturday."

Janie Jameson
@LadyThreat

Barely working this Saturday

DARKO

TROJAN

Sally Sanders
@CurrentGirlfriend

@LadyThreat wait that's my
boyfriend's place

dated my college boyfriend for a year and a half.
Three months after graduation, we had been doing
long distance, and I thought everything had been going
great.

On Halloween, he picked me up from a party in
Detroit and we drove back to Ann Arbor for a
friend's party. We hung out with his friends for a
while and then went upstairs. After sleeping together,
he immediately broke up with me out of nowhere. He
said he just couldn't do the distance anymore. All of
the problems in our relationship surfaced, including him
accusing me of not liking his friends (which I told him
-- well, I don't). All of this was through lots of tears
and drunk emotions. Plus, I was stuck in his house on
Halloween and there was a giant party going on
downstairs.

At 3 a.m. I decided I wasn't going to be trapped in his
room for the night and made him drive me back to
Cleveland. I sat in the back seat for the two-and-a-
half-hour drive and we didn't say a word. When I got

out of the car he said "I'll never forget you," to which I replied "Have a good life."

I walked into my house and haven't spoken to him since. About a week after we broke up he sent me a letter saying how much our relationship meant to him. He also said "I'm so happy our lives crossed, I think they are going to cross again." Needless to say, our lives definitely aren't crossing again.

HOW MUCH TO REVEAL

zero   I ♡ cheese   crazy

A white guy I was dating broke up with me after two months. It took him that long to realize that I was not Latino.

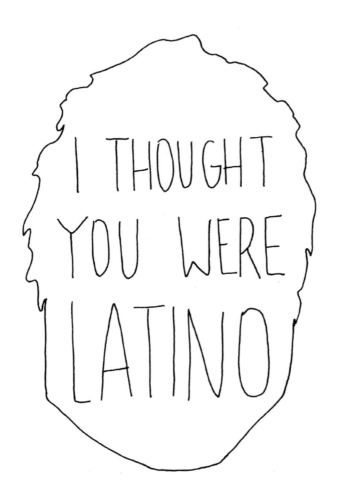

When I was a freshman in college, I had an epiphany that I had my whole life ahead of me and a world of choices. So I decided to break up with my high school boyfriend. We had only been dating four months, so I didn't think it would be that big a deal.

We met up in person and I was very honest with him. I was very supportive and upbeat, reassuring him that it wasn't goodbye forever, just a natural changing of course in our lives. Then he started having heart palpitations. At first I thought he was being dramatic... nope. I called an ambulance because he was having all the symptoms of a heart attack.

A week later, he was recovering from his episode (it was like a mild heart attack, not a real one) and my mom told his mom that I was trying to break up with him, which she then mentioned to him. He was like, "What? She was trying to break up with me?" And there he was again dropping to the floor, suffering from heart failure. It was impossible to break up with this guy.

IF YOU LEAVE ME I WILL DIE

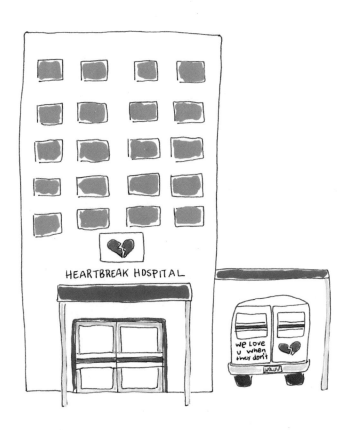

I was pretty heavily obsessed with a guy, enough to convince me to move across the country. The months leading up to the move were great. We had constant contact with each other and got along so well that I was blinded by the potential of a new boyfriend.

I ignored it when he dropped off the map two weeks before my arrival. I ignored it when my questioning of the dropping of the map resulted in bland, vague, evasive texts.

But when I arrived in my new home and he continued to be distant, I asked him outright if he didn't want to see me. He replied, "I swear I'm really busy. I can show you my calendar if you want."

I SWEAR I'M REALLY BUSY

I CAN SHOW YOU MY CALENDAR

IF YOU WANT

was 13 and going out with a girl from another school. Her name was - of course, being a middle school cool girl - Courtney. I didn't think I had a chance with her in the first place. I was acting as though it wasn't a big deal, but was secretly anxious that she'd figure out I wasn't cool enough at any second.

I think we dated for two months, two-and-a-half, tops. Then one day I went to hockey practice and saw some friends who went to the same middle school as Courtney. At some point during the typical pre-practice chatter and latest grade school gossip, my friend Adam (who was very impressed when I started to date Courtney) asked me a question from across the locker room.

"Hey man, how's things with you and Courtney?"
I looked up from tying my skates and thought I'd act like we broke up as a joke - just to throw him.
"Aww man, we actually broke up..." I paused here, anticipating his shocked reaction. "I know, man, she

told me. I'm sorry about that," he replied with feeling. "What?" I said, shocked. "I was just joking! What do you mean she told you?"

"Oooooooooooooooooohhhhh," everyone wailed.

I don't remember much else, other than pestering Adam for details he wouldn't divulge because "it wasn't his place."

NOTHING LASTS

We had been dating for over a year. After a minor argument left me sobbing into the very expensive dinner I had saved up to treat him to, the following took place:

Me: "Do you think our relationship has an expiration date?"

Him, without hesitation: "Yes."

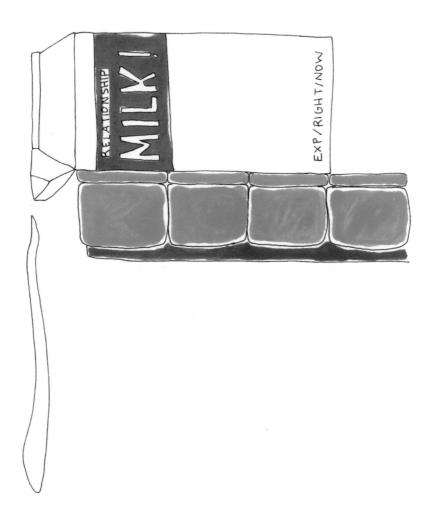

RELATIONSHIP MILK! EXP/RIGHT/NOW

asked Joanne to go steady during a lunch break in the fall of 1967. A few months earlier, she included me on a semi-exclusive birthday party list. It was my first coed gathering. So, using the unrefined logic of an eighth-grade male, I concluded this was a clear sign she would go steady with me. I was one of those middle-schoolers who was super bold when asking a girl onto the dance floor, but this was foreign territory.

In fact, she did accept the navy blue varsity jacket on that Thursday afternoon. She cheerfully put the jacket on and suggested I call her that evening. Coming from a big family, I secured the one private phone in the house for the after-dinner call. It was in my father's home office, which had an entrance from the garage that my seven siblings rarely used. I compiled a list of talking points to avoid the panic of phone silence. Our 20-minute conversation went well, but halfway through the call I had depleted my entire list of topics. Plus, we never discussed the weekend. Isn't that what couples do, make plans for the weekend?

JOANNE DOESN'T WANT TO GO STEADY ANYMORE

I didn't see Joanne at school the next day. The final bell rang and I boarded the bus early. Staring out the window, I brainstormed possible weekend activities; a bike ride, a matinee, maybe a picnic (even though I had never been on a picnic). Yes, I would call Joanne once I got home and make some plans.

Joanne's best friend, a girl named Trudi, stepped onto the bus. This wasn't her regular bus. Perhaps she had a message to deliver from Joanne, I thought. She glanced down the rows and spotted me. She strolled toward me with calculated nonchalance. I noticed she was clutching a varsity jacket. With a stoic, calm voice, she said, "Joanne wanted me to return this to you. She doesn't want to go steady anymore."

She handed me the navy blue varsity jacket like a borrowed library book and quickly exited the bus. Luckily, Trudi's discretion avoided any possible drama; none of the kids appeared to notice the returned jacket, or my Friday afternoon surrogate breakup.

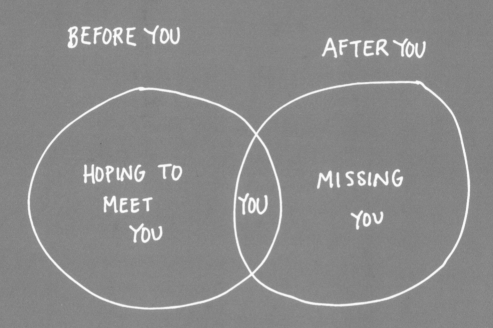

decided to throw a huge surprise birthday party for my long distance girlfriend.

I flew two of her friends in from Vegas and Monterey and worked with her best friend for a month to organize everything. I was so thrilled with my plans that I didn't notice how aloof she was when I arrived in SoCal the day before.

As we were stuck in L.A. traffic on the way to the party, she confessed to cheating for the last six months and said she wanted to end our relationship. When we got to her house, I not only had to put on a brave face, but I also learned that the person she had been cheating on me with was her best friend... the very one who helped me plan the party.

My girlfriend and I wound up going to separate colleges and our lives just naturally went in different directions. We stayed together for her first year, which was my second, even when I realized we hadn't talked in a full month.

We spent a lot of time together the summer after, when we were both home. But a week before we headed back to school, we acknowledged that, realistically, we wouldn't see each other much in the future. We both planned on staying in our college towns the following summers.

We were both a little bummed but knew it was for the best.

So I said, "It's probably time we called it splitzies." She said, "I can't believe you just said 'splitzies.'"

I replied, "I think you know me well enough to know that I would say 'splitzies.'"

"Everyone is always saying what a great guy you are," my ex-girlfriend said one day. I turned my face to hers and smiled.

But she wasn't finished. "After all this time with you," she continued, "I'm still waiting to meet that guy they're talking about."

Ouch.

SHOW ME WHERE IT HURTS

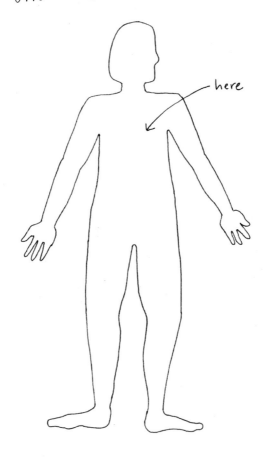

here

My long-distance boyfriend and I were in the middle of a fight and he was not speaking to me. I decided the best way to get his attention would be to freak him out, so I texted him that my period was late, which was true.

When he called me, very concerned, I told him that yes, I was late but he didn't really have to worry that much. It might not be his. Also true.

My plan didn't work - we never spoke again.

In first grade, Darryl was my boyfriend. He told me that he didn't like my hair in a ponytail, and if I wore one again he'd break up with me. Cut to next day: my mom is painfully yanking my hair back into a ponytail. The kind where your hair is pulled back so tight that your eyes slant back toward your ears.

Sure enough, at recess, Darryl broke up with me. I'm wearing a ponytail as I type this, but it took me a long time to feel attractive with one.

DAY 1

If you wear your hair in a pony tail again I'll break up with you

 DAY 2

Her: "Dan, I think I need more space."

Me: "I haven't seen you in a year and a half,
          how much more space could you need?"

(Pointed silence.)

Me: "Oh."

Are you like,
"OMG I have a story!"?

Submissions for
"Breaking Up Is Hard To Do,
But You Could've Done Better"
remain open at cartoonsbyhilary.com
(until people stop being so terrible).

THE CARTOONIST WISHES TO THANK THESE PEOPLE
SPECIFICALLY BUT IN NO SPECIFIC ORDER

Everyone who shared their heartbreak
with me, without you there would be no
book.

Laurie Campbell, for being my mom.

Doug Campbell, for being my dad.

Anna Germinidi, for telling me that the
first title for this project was a little
aggressive.

Kristin Molloy, for letting me scan art at
her work among so many other things.

Beth Prouty, for getting my shit together.

Steve Hoover, for thinking I could turn
this into a book.

Derek Boeckelmann, for enduring my
insanity and in such close proximity.

Photo by Kristen Bartley

ABOUT THE ARTIST

Hilary Fitzgerald Campbell is an award winning cartoonist and documentary filmmaker residing in Brooklyn, NY. Her films "This Is Not The End" and "Small Talk" have played in festivals across the country, including Slamdance, Rooftop Films and more. She is the creator of Cartoons by Hilary, a popular daily cartoon series on Instagram (@cartoonsbyhilary).

Campbell's work has appeared in Cosmopolitan and The Huffington Post. She co-illustrated Jessica Bennett's critically acclaimed "Feminist Fight Club." "Breaking Up Is Hard To Do, But You Could've Done Better" is her first published book of cartoons.

You can see more of her work at cartoonsbyhilary.com.